D1233176

Robotics Engineer

Other titles in the *Cutting Edge Careers* series include:

Big Data Analyst

Cybersecurity Analyst

Software Engineer

Video Game Designer

Virtual Reality Developer

Robotics
Engineer

Kathryn Hulick

ReferencePoint Press®

San Diego, CA

DEC 5 – 2017

© 2018 ReferencePoint Press, Inc.
Printed in the United States

For more information, contact:
ReferencePoint Press, Inc.
PO Box 27779
San Diego, CA 92198
www.ReferencePointPress.com

ALL RIGHTS RESERVED.
No part of this work covered by the copyright hereon may be reproduced or used in any form or by any means—graphic, electronic, or mechanical, including photocopying, recording, taping, web distribution, or information storage retrieval systems—without the written permission of the publisher.

LIBRARY OF CONGRESS CATALOGING-IN-PUBLICATION DATA

Name: Hulick, Kathryn, author.
Title: Robotics Engineer/by Kathryn Hulick.
Other titles: Cutting Edge careers.
Description: San Diego, CA : ReferencePoint Press, Inc., 2018. | Series: Cutting edge careers | Audience: Grades 9 to 12. | Includes bibliographical references and index.
Identifiers: LCCN 2016055894 (print) | LCCN 2016058107 (ebook) | ISBN 9781682821862 (hardback) | ISBN 9781682821879 (eBook)
Subjects: LCSH: Robotics--Vocational guidance--Juvenile literature. | Robots--Design and construction--Juvenile literature. | CYAC: Vocational guidance.
Classification: LCC TJ211.2 .H85 2018 (print) | LCC TJ211.2 (ebook) | DDC 629.8/92--dc23
LC record available at https://lccn.loc.gov/2016055894

CONTENTS

ROBOTICS ENGINEER AT A GLANCE

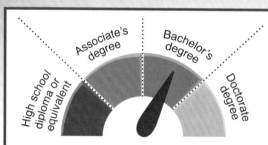

Minimum Educational Requirements

High school diploma or equivalent · Associate's degree · Bachelor's degree · Doctorate degree

Working Conditions

Indoors

Personal Qualities

- ☑ Problem solving
- ☑ Creativity
- ☑ Attention to detail
- ☑ Strong science, math, and computer-programming skills

Median Salary — **$81,591**

278,000*

Number of jobs

*Numbers are for mechanical engineers, a group that includes robotics engineers.

Percent job increase by 2024

5%

Future Job Outlook

Source: Bureau of Labor Statistics, *Occupational Outlook Handbook*. www.bls.gov.

Turning Science Fiction into Reality

In the *Star Wars* movies, the robots (called droids) R2-D2, C-3PO, BB-8, and K-2SO keep secrets, face danger, and help save the day. Real robots have a long way to go before they become such lifelike companions. But robotics engineers are working to make such a future a reality.

Robotics technology is advancing at a breakneck pace. Today there are robots that just a few years ago were the stuff of science fiction and fantasy. For example, all new Tesla cars now come with a self-driving mode. In warehouses teams of Kiva robots work together to find, fetch, and carry items that customers order. A robot called DRC-HUBO, the winner of the 2015 DARPA Robotics Challenge, can drive a vehicle, open a door, turn a valve, operate a drill, cross through a pile of rubble, and climb stairs. In the past it would have been realistic to expect a robot to do one or two of those things—but not all of them.

The research firm Tractica expects the market for robots to quadruple between 2015 and 2020. Most of the jobs in this growing industry will go to engineers. In 2012 *Forbes* magazine placed robotics second on a list of top majors that college students should consider. The fact that the population is aging and there are not enough young people to serve in the labor force is one factor driving this need. "This creates a demand for personal services that simply can't be met—and robots will fill the void," explains author Alex Knapp. Over the coming years, industries ranging from health care to transportation will become increasingly dependent on robots. Knapp says, "This will create a huge need for people in the robotics industry, from programming to engineering."[1]

A Robotics Revolution

The robotics industry divides its products into two groups: industrial robots and service robots. Industrial robots have been around since the 1960s, when they were introduced to put cars together on assembly lines. Today industrial robots help make all kinds of products. Typically, each industrial robot is programmed to perform a specific task. For example, it might cut, bend, inspect, weld, or move objects from place to place.

While the market for industrial robots is expected to grow steadily, the market for service robots is exploding. Service robots are those that do anything other than manufacturing. Examples include robots that perform chores such as vacuuming or farming. Service robots also assist people who have disabilities or illnesses and help doctors perform surgery. Construction robots, surveillance drones, bomb disposal robots, and space exploration rovers are also included in this group. Such robots have the potential to further science and greatly improve people's quality of life. For example, "the advent of personal service robots means that the elderly can live longer on their own before going to retirement homes,"[2] says Knapp.

> "As I look at the trends that are now starting to converge, I can envision a future in which robotic devices will become a nearly ubiquitous part of our day-to-day lives."[5]
>
> —Bill Gates, cofounder of Microsoft

Robots are taking over tasks that people either dislike or should not have to perform. "Anytime there's an environment that's dull, dirty, or dangerous for a human being, you'll need a robot," says Daniel H. Wilson, author of *How to Survive a Robot Uprising*. "That's why we send robots into outer space, war zones, and active volcanoes."[3] Erik Nieves, founder of PlusOne Robotics, adds that in manufacturing, robots perform tasks such as welding, grinding, sanding, and stacking, all jobs that are dangerous and physically demanding. "Let's use robots to do those kinds of tasks and free up people to do work where they can use their mind and creativity,"[4] he says.

Bill Gates, cofounder of Microsoft, and other experts have predicted that the robot revolution will change people's lives as

The DRC-HUBO robot, pictured turning a valve during a disaster response demonstration, is an example of the dramatic advances that are driving the robotics field and creating a rich source of job opportunities for robotics engineers.

much as the computer and Internet revolutions did. "As I look at the trends that are now starting to converge, I can envision a future in which robotic devices will become a nearly ubiquitous part of our day-to-day lives,"[5] said Gates in 2007. A decade later, it is difficult to imagine *not* using computers and the Internet to conduct business or communicate with others. Though robots are not yet in every home and business, they likely will be soon.

The Future Belongs to Engineers

It is up to the engineers of today and tomorrow to make that future a reality. Robotics is an emerging field, but one that combines a variety of traditional engineering skills. Chris Jones, director for research advancement at iRobot, describes the field as being a mix of core subjects. "Robotics . . . brings together many disciplines—electrical engineering, mechanical engineering, system engineering, computer science and even psychology gets pulled in to help figure how robots can interact with people around them."[6]

Those who want to work on robots must develop a wide and varied skill set. Because of the highly technical education required, people with these skills can be hard to find. Anne Fisher of *Fortune* magazine writes, "The shortage of people who know how to build, program, maintain, and repair robots has gotten so severe that, in some parts of the country, qualified candidates can practically write their own ticket."[7] In the past, robotics engineering degrees were rare. Now an increasing number of students are focusing their studies in this field. Robotics engineers can expect to earn high salaries and have the potential to work in a variety of different industries, including health care, the military, energy, and entertainment.

More importantly, though, robotics engineers are building our future. "As an engineer, our job is to come up with new ideas and new inventions to help us explore the universe, help us learn about the world, and make the world a better place," says Paulo Younse, a robotics engineer at the National Aeronautics and Space Administration Jet Propulsion Laboratory (NASA JPL). "It is our job to take the lead and inspire the world to follow."[8]

CHAPTER 1

What Does a Robotics Engineer Do?

Robotics engineers make robots. They design and build new robots or test and maintain robots currently in operation. Engineering is all about solving problems, and robotics engineering is no exception. The robotics engineering process begins by identifying a problem that a robot could solve. For example, a warehouse may need a team of robots that can locate and gather items to complete a customer's order. Then a team of engineers will work together to design such a robot, or customize an existing one for that particular situation. The engineers plan out designs or simulations on a computer before building the physical robot. They also build prototypes—rough draft physical models—before taking a solution to production. The team tests the simulations and prototypes thoroughly to make sure they work as expected.

Glitches, mistakes, and even crashes often occur during the design and testing process. Robotics engineers must work as a team to identify and solve these problems. A team of robotics engineers contains people who specialize in different traditional engineering fields, including mechanical engineering, electrical engineering, and software engineering. Controls engineers, test engineers, systems engineers, and industrial engineers may also contribute to a robot's design and development. Each expert has a special role to play in bringing a robot to life.

Building a Mechanical Body and Brain

Robotics engineers who specialize in mechanical engineering determine which materials are best for each part of the robot and how these parts will work together. For example, the engineers need to make sure that joints—the parts that connect a robot's arms and legs together—will bear weight correctly. They must also make sure that heat from the robot's motion and electrical power will transfer through the robot's body without damaging any components. They also troubleshoot failures in its mechanical system.

Electrical engineering brings the robot to life. Just as a person's blood vessels carry energy and oxygen around the body, a robot's wires and circuits carry electricity to all of its components. This powers the robot as it moves and performs tasks. Robotics engineers who focus on electrical systems also design and integrate sensor systems. These allow a robot to take in information from its environment. For example, a robot may need a camera and a Global Positioning System receiver to navigate or infrared sensors to detect heat.

Even if a robot is great at moving and gathering information from its environment, it is useless unless it is able to accomplish something productive. This is where software engineering and programming come in. A robotics engineer who works on software is responsible for writing the computer programs that form a robot's brain. These programs tell the robot how to interact with its environment, from basic to more advanced levels. The software

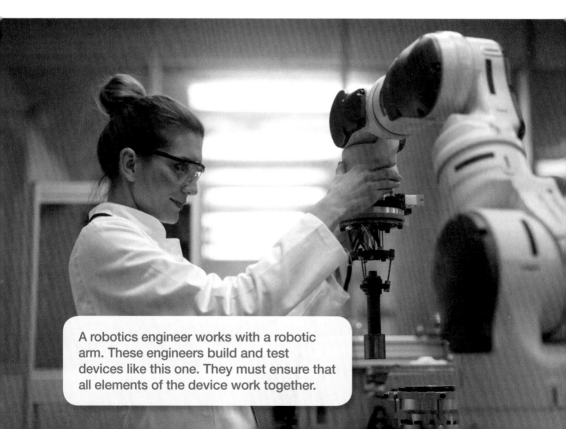

A robotics engineer works with a robotic arm. These engineers build and test devices like this one. They must ensure that all elements of the device work together.

also allows a human user to input customized commands or train a robot to perform a specific task.

Putting It All Together

Designing and building a robot's body and brain is an important part of a robotics engineer's job. However, these are not the only tasks these engineers are responsible for. Robotics engineers may also do controls engineering. In this role, they make a robot able to modify its own actions using feedback from its sensors, or they may develop other controls to improve its performance. For example, walking robots must traverse unfamiliar environments. The robot's feet will not always hit the ground in the exact same position or with the same force. This can result in the robot falling over if its control systems are unable to adjust with each new step.

Robotics engineers also do a lot of testing. If a robot falls over, gets physically stuck, or has a program crash, the engineer must troubleshoot the problem and ensure it does not happen again. Some engineers specialize in designing tests for robots to make sure they perform as expected. At iRobot, a company that makes vacuum-cleaning robots, test engineers set the robots loose in a lab that contains things the robots might encounter in a person's home, such as different kinds of flooring. If the robot keeps getting stuck on thick carpet, for example, the test engineer will work with the rest of the engineering team to devise a solution.

Finally, robotics engineers make sure all of the components of a robot or robotics system work together smoothly. An industrial engineer focuses on the practical application of a system, while a systems engineer focuses on the overall design. Both roles troubleshoot problems and modify the robot to increase efficiency.

Industrial Robots

Traditionally, most jobs in robotics have focused on producing industrial robots for manufacturing, especially automobile production. Though a lot of robotics engineers still work in this field, many other industries are beginning to use robots. Today robotics engineers may work in agriculture, construction, law enforcement, the military, manufacturing, education, entertainment, health care, mining, utilities and energy, warehouses, and space or deep-sea exploration. According to Marcia O'Malley, associate professor of mechanical engineering and materials science at Rice University, "There are great opportunities for robotics engineers with oil and gas (remote underwater vehicles); with NASA Johnson Space Center . . . and even opportunities in medical robotics and rehabilitation robotics."[9]

However, industrial robots remain the most common kind of robot used in the world today. An industrial robot performs a specific task on a factory assembly line or in a warehouse. According to the International Federation of Robotics, 2.3 million robots will operate on factory floors worldwide by 2018, doubling the number of robots that were deployed in 2009. All of these robots were designed by engineers and must be kept up-to-date by them, too.

Industrial robotics companies include ABB Robotics, which supplies robots for manufacturing tasks, and Aethon, which develops mobile robots to transport, deliver, and track materials. Traditional industrial robots cannot sense their environment and simply follow programmed instructions. A person getting in the robot's way could be injured, so most industrial robots are enclosed in cages. However, a new generation of robots can sense their surroundings and is being built to collaborate safely with humans to learn tasks. Rethink Robotics is one example of a company producing collaborative robots.

> "There are great opportunities for robotics engineers with oil and gas (remote underwater vehicles); with NASA Johnson Space Center . . . and even opportunities in medical robotics and rehabilitation robotics."[9]
>
> —Marcia O'Malley, professor at Rice University

Medical and Household Robots

The medical industry is growing at an incredible pace in the United States, and robotics engineers are therefore working on robots that assist with surgery, rehabilitation, or even nursing duties. "In the next few years, thousands of 'service robots' are expected to enter the healthcare sector," writes *Wall Street Journal* reporter

A Jack-of-All-Trades

In the engineering world, a robotics engineer is a jack-of-all-trades. An education in robotics helps a person develop skills in mechanical engineering, electrical engineering, software engineering, and more. However, once a robotics engineering student enters the workforce, he or she usually specializes in a traditional engineering role within the robotics industry.

For example, Ty Tremblay has a master's degree in robotics engineering but works as a field systems engineer at the robotics company Symbotic. However, he considers himself a robotics engineer at heart and loves being able to understand so many different engineering disciplines. "I can speak the language of any engineer in the company, which I think is really powerful," he says. "I can walk up to the mechanical engineers and discuss why they chose this certain bolt and then in the same day go to the software engineer and talk about messaging architecture. It makes solving problems within the company easier for me."

Ty Tremblay, interview with the author, June 21, 2016.

Timothy Hay. "Picture R2-D2 from Star Wars carrying a tray of medications or a load of laundry down hospital corridors."[10]

Medical robots include those that assist with surgery. In robotic surgery the surgeon typically sits at a computer and uses a joystick to control a robotic arm to perform a procedure. Cameras show the surgeon detailed views of the surgery site. Nursing robots lift and move patients who are too ill to walk or fetch items such as food and medication.

Household robots include cuddly, pet-like robots designed to provide comfort and companionship to the elderly. In rehabilitation, engineers are designing robotic arms and legs for people who are paralyzed or have lost a limb. Researchers are even experimenting with systems that allow a paralyzed patient to operate a robotic arm with brain activity alone.

Robots are popular in service industries as well. Some hotels use robots to bring items to guests. Schools are bringing robots into the classroom to teach programming or foreign languages. Robots can help students with autism or other learning disorders communicate with others or focus on tasks. In the home, robots can do all sorts of chores. The Roomba, a vacuum-cleaning robot, was one of the first to make its way to consumers. Now people can also buy a robotic lawn mower, an alarm clock that scuttles away if you try to turn it off, and a robotic cat litter cleaner. Basically, if there is a chore you do not like doing, chances are, a robotics engineer is out there building a robot to do it for you.

While robots as sophisticated and person-like as R2-D2 and C-3PO are not yet an everyday reality, there are virtual assistants such as Siri on the iPhone and Alexa on the Amazon Echo. These computer programs take voice commands to perform searches, play music, or text a friend. Technically, they are not robots because they do not move through space, but the artificial intelligence software that runs these assistants could easily be installed in a robot companion.

Robots for Exploration and Beyond

Some of the robots that engineers build are not even meant to be used on this planet. Ayanna Howard, who works for NASA JPL, is working on the next generation of rover-style robots to explore other worlds. "What I'm working on is to allow rovers to travel long distances on the surface of Mars," she says. Her team wants the robot to be able to recognize a destination, such as a distant mountain, then plan a path to get there. To do that, she says, "we have to have the robots think intelligently and be able to navigate by themselves, alone, on Mars."[11] Here on Earth, scientists use robots to explore the deep sea, and energy companies use them to seek out oil and gas deposits. "Engineers foresee a day when fully automated rigs roll onto a job site using satellite coordinates, erect 14-story-tall steel reinforcements on their own, drill a well, then pack up and move to the next site,"[12] says reporter David Wethe in an article on the Bloomberg website.

"What I'm working on is to allow rovers to travel long distances on the surface of Mars."[11]

—Ayanna Howard, robotics engineer at NASA JPL

In agriculture, robots assist with harvesting, pruning, weeding, sorting, and more. In the military and law enforcement, robotic drones carry out surveillance. Robots can also seek and defuse explosives, and researchers are developing robots to perform search-and-rescue missions. Companies such as General Dynamics, ReconRobotics, Raytheon, and Lockheed Martin hire robotics engineers to produce robots for the military. Finally, self-driving cars are technically robots. Companies such as Tesla, Google, Toyota, and BMW are working to make these robotic vehicles part of our everyday lives.

CHAPTER 2

How Do You Become a Robotics Engineer?

Robotics engineering is a multidisciplinary field, so people working in this career come from a range of academic backgrounds. A bachelor's or advanced degree in math, science, computer science, or almost any engineering field can lead to a career in robotics. While degree programs specifically designed around robotics engineering are becoming more popular, most of these programs are for graduate students.

If an undergraduate or graduate degree is not affordable, many vocational schools and community colleges provide two-year associate's degree programs in robotics or automation. While this degree will not land you a job as an engineer, it could get you in the door as a robotics technician. From there, you should be able to gain enough experience and additional training to eventually work your way into an engineering position.

Math, Physics, and Computer Science

You can start preparing for a career in robotics while in high school by taking advanced courses in math, physics, computer science, and computer-aided design (CAD) or computer-aided manufacturing (CAM). Of these, math is the most essential subject to master. All engineers rely on mathematical formulas and equations to solve problems. Mathematical concepts also underlie much of computer science and programming. Along these lines, Erik Nieves's advice for kids interested in robotics is to "pay attention in math class."[13]

According to Nieves, math and physics classes prepared him most for his career as a robotics engineer. He uses geometry and linear algebra every day. "Geometry is very important in robotics," he says. "Robots are essentially machines that move, and those motions are described in a language of geometry. . . . When robots don't behave correctly, you need to go back and look at your linear algebra." Courses in physics were also very helpful to Nieves. "That's where I learned about friction, torque, inertia, leverage, and a lot of mechanical properties that make up robots today."[14]

A background in computer science and programming, or writing code, is also important. In robotics, code is what allows a robot to accomplish tasks. Arin Morfopoulos, a robotics engineer at NASA JPL, says that one of the most useful classes he took as a student was on programming. "Programming is a pretty essential skill for robotics," writes Alex Owen-Hill, a writer who has a PhD in telerobotics, a field concerned with controlling robots at a distance, usually through a wireless network. "It

A student makes adjustments to a robot. Many students who have an interest in robotics get good experience by taking part in school robotics clubs and competitions.

doesn't matter if you're involved in low-level control systems . . . or if you're a computer scientist designing high-level cognitive systems."[15]

Interestingly, robots themselves are becoming a trendy new tool for teaching programming concepts to kids. Many schools have started using commercially available programmable robots to introduce computer science to students as early as elementary school. Examples include Dash and Dot, Sphero, and NAO. If you have access to one of these robots or to a robotics tool kit such as LEGO Mindstorms or VEX Robotics, jump right in and play around. You will learn important lessons about robotics and computer programming, too.

The College Experience

Undergraduate degree programs that prepare a student for robotics engineering include classes in mechanical, electrical, and software engineering. Mechanical engineering classes introduce concepts such as kinematics, the study of motion and forces that cause motion, and thermodynamics, which is the study of how heat and energy are transferred. Electrical engineering includes courses in the components of electrical circuits, and software engineering includes computer science and programming classes. Finally, some students may be able to take classes entirely on robotics. A robotics class may cover control systems or programmable logic systems for directing robots. It may also cover CAD or CAM, which are used to design robots. The class may also cover the principles of hydraulics and pneumatics to make the robot move. A robot with a hydraulic system would depend on the motion of water or another liquid through pipes to generate motion. A pneumatic system uses a gas rather than a liquid.

Undergraduate programs devoted solely to robotics are relatively rare, so it is often best to pursue a bachelor's degree in mechanical engineering and concentrate in robotics. Marcia O'Malley describes what these programs teach students: "Mechanical and robotic engineering students learn how to approach a problem, generate solutions, evaluate solutions and support their decisions with engineering fundamentals."[16]

If your undergraduate program of choice does not offer robotics courses, do not worry. "Any college or university with an engineering program can put you on the path towards a career in robotics,"[17] says Rich Hooper, a robotics engineer and consultant who designs and builds custom robots. After earning a bachelor's degree in engineering, someone who is interested in robotics should consider getting a master's degree or even a PhD. Getting an advanced degree offers the opportunity to specialize in a particular area of the field, such as artificial intelligence or robots used for medical purposes. This opens up doors to a variety of interesting positions that are on the cutting edge of robotics.

At Johns Hopkins University in Baltimore, Maryland, students in the robotics master's degree program can pick one of six areas to focus on. They can choose automation science and engineering, which looks at CAD, mechatronics, and kinematics. Or they might like biorobotics, in which they will explore locomotion and the physics of living systems. Another choice is control and dynamical systems, which involves mathematical modeling and control theory. Medical robotics and computer-integrated surgical systems focus on medical imaging, robot sensors, and machine learning, while perception and cognitive systems explore artificial intelligence, computer vision, and image processing and analysis. Alternatively, students can just focus on general robotics.

> "Any college or university with an engineering program can put you on the path towards a career in robotics."[17]
>
> —Rich Hooper, robotics engineer and consultant

Other colleges and universities with excellent robotics programs include Carnegie Mellon University, the University of California–Berkeley, Georgia Institute of Technology, Stanford University, Massachusetts Institute of Technology (MIT), and Worcester Polytechnic Institute (WPI). All of these schools run institutes, centers, or laboratories devoted to research and development in robotics.

Almost all robotics engineers working in research and development at government agencies such as NASA or at colleges and universities have advanced degrees or are working on earning them. Edward Tunstel got hired by NASA JPL after completing a master's degree. He went on to earn a PhD in electrical engineering with a focus on mobile robot control systems and navigation. "[My degree] better prepared me to perform independent research at NASA based on my own ideas and lead teams of engineers in making new ideas become reality," he says. He suggests that for students interested in robotics, "advanced degrees will allow more control over what projects they work on and increase the opportunities for applying more of their own creativity."[18]

Internships

While in college or graduate school, robotics engineering students should seek out internships. "[Robotics] is a very hot field right now, so there are a lot of internship opportunities,"[19] says Joseph St. Germain, the robotics lab manager at WPI. An internship can help a student get a foot in the door in the industry and may even lead to a full-time job offer. One example of an internship program is NASA's Robotics Academy program. This ten-week internship assigns participants to work on a project with NASA, a local industry, or an academic institution. Morfopoulos completed an internship with NASA. He says that he learned more as an intern than he did in school.

> I spent most of my time learning to do: how to solder and build electronics from scratch, how to write code in a large software environment, and how to test your software to make sure it actually worked and didn't just fail or crash! It was an amazing environment because I was working in a lab full of other engineers with such diverse skill sets that whenever I touched on a subject there was an expert standing right there. I couldn't overstate the importance that being an intern had upon my abilities as an engineer.[20]

Robotics Competitions

Most people go into robotics because they love tinkering with machinery and computers. They enjoy figuring out how to make a robot behave a certain way. While math and science classes lay

Inside a Robotics Engineering Degree Program

Worcester Polytechnic Institute in Massachusetts was the first university in the United States to offer an undergraduate degree in robotics engineering. Joseph St. Germain manages the robotics lab at WPI. He says the major is one of the more difficult ones at the school. "It takes more effort, more time, and a dedicated person to complete it," he notes.

To earn the degree, students must design and build a real robot. These range from autonomous vehicles to robots that assist in surgery, manufacturing, and entertainment. Students are responsible for conceptualizing, designing, implementing, evaluating, and writing up documentation for the robot. They must also take into account issues such as ethics, environmental impacts, sustainability, aesthetics, and safety. Required courses for the degree include the following:

- Robotics engineering
- Computer science
- Electrical and computer engineering
- Mathematics
- Physics
- Entrepreneurship
- Social implications of technology

Joseph St. Germain, interview with the author, June 11, 2016.

the foundation for a career in robotics, the most valuable lessons come from hands-on experience. Robotics clubs and competitions give kids and teens the opportunity to design, build, and test robots as part of a team.

Many robotics engineers fell in love with robots thanks to these competitions. This is what happened for Fernando Zumbado, a robotics systems engineer at NASA. When he was an undergraduate student at Northwestern University, he went to a robotics competition the school held each year. That particular year, the robots had to find their way through a maze. He intended to just look around for a little while, but he ended up staying for the entire competition. "I was consumed by all the different solutions the teams had conjured for the maze they needed to navigate," he said. "Shortly after, I enrolled in robotics courses in the engineering school and chose robotics as the concentration for my mechanical engineering degree."[21]

Ty Tremblay also chose a career in robotics after stumbling, literally, into a robotics competition while he was in high school. "I was running late one day and took a shortcut through a place where a high school FIRST robotics team was practicing. They lost control of their robot. It ran me over, and pinned me up against the wall."[22] This surprising encounter wound up inspiring him to join the team, and he eventually gave up his former goal of becoming a chef to focus on robotics instead.

"Tinkering with computers, robots, video games, etc. is a good use of time since you never really stop doing similar things in a career as a robotics engineer."[24]

—Edward Tunstel, robotics engineer at NASA JPL

Robotics competitions are offered internationally for students in kindergarten through college and beyond. One is the Wonder League Robotics Competition, which invites kids ages six to twelve to program and enhance Dash and Dot robots in order to complete challenges. In the FIRST Robotics Competition, teams of high school students get six weeks to build a robot that must play a game against other teams' robots. FIRST LEGO League offers similar competitions for elementary and middle school students. VEX Robotics Competitions are open to kids in elementary, middle, and high school. Once in college or a university, students may compete in adult engineering competitions such as the US Department of Defense's DARPA Robotics Challenge.

All of these competitions challenge participants to solve problems that involve science, technology, engineering, and math. They give students valuable hands-on experience building, programming, and fixing robots. Ethan Schaezler, a sixteen-year-old student, first learned to write computer code when he participated in FIRST LEGO League in elementary school. The LEGO NXT Brick is a small computer that gives instructions to a LEGO robot. It has its own programming language called NXT-G. "With NXT-G, I was introduced to and familiarized with numerous programming concepts such as loops, conditional statements, etc.," says Schaezler. "Additionally, I learned a substantial amount of things pertaining to the logic that is used for programming robots."[23]

No matter what educational path you pursue, if you love robots, it is a good idea to start building and programming robots now. "Tinkering with computers, robots, video games, etc. is a good use of time since you never really stop doing similar things in a career as a robotics engineer,"[24] says Edward Tunstel. Most middle and high schools host robotics clubs or competitions. Robotics hardware kits, controllers, and simple programmable robots are available at a range of prices. Robotics software can also be found online for free. Finally, some schools provide access to 3D printers, which can be valuable tools for producing custom parts for a robot.

CHAPTER 3

What Skills and Personal Qualities Matter Most—and Why?

First and foremost, robotics engineers must be very good problem solvers. They must have sufficient technical skill to recognize and understand a problem and enough creativity to think up an original solution. Robotics engineers must also pay close attention to detail—it takes focused dedication to solve difficult engineering problems. People in this career typically enjoy math, science, technology, and figuring out how things work. They may spend their spare time taking apart machines and putting them back together again.

Robotics engineers should also have a passion for robots and machines in general. "You have to have a lot of drive and really care about what you're doing,"[25] says Corey Russell, a test engineer at iRobot. He explains that robotics engineers must sometimes work long hours to diagnose a problem or must implement a solution under a tight deadline. If an engineer loves what he or she does, putting in the extra time and energy the job requires is much easier.

Tackling Problems with Creativity and Persistence

Whether a robotics engineer focuses on electrical, mechanical, or software engineering or on some other aspect of robotics, he or she will spend most days troubleshooting problems and developing solutions. This includes foreseeing problems before they occur. Eugene Kozlenko, a mechanical engineer who works on robotic limbs, is constantly coming up with creative solutions to problems. "You can't go more than a few hours without having to come up with something clever," he says. "Whether it's the most cost-effective way to machine [build] a particular part, or coming up with a way to test a circuit that narrows down which component is acting up—every day is full of little opportunities."[26]

Thinking outside the box allows an engineer to come up with new, creative ideas every day. Paying strict attention to detail makes it possible to carefully analyze those ideas and plan a well-thought-out solution. Judgment and decision-making skills help navigate the numerous choices that go into designing or maintaining a robot.

Sometimes, however, a problem may seem too daunting. Or solution after solution might fail to fix the problem. It is at this point that a robotics engineer must have extreme patience and determination. He or she must be able to soldier on even when everything seems to be going wrong. Often, what separates an average engineer from a great one is the ability to persevere in the face of failure and frustration. "You have to keep a cool head when things don't work because quite a lot of times they do not," says Kozlenko. "I had a professor that told me to fail as often as possible because that's how you learn, and that's very true in robotics."[27]

Winola Lenore Rasmussen agrees. She is a computer science professor at WPI. She also owns a robotics company, Ras Labs, that produces synthetic muscles. She says it is important for robotics engineers not to get frustrated. "You learn as much from what doesn't work as what does work,"[28] she notes.

> "You can't go more than a few hours without having to come up with something clever. Whether it's the most cost-effective way to machine [build] a particular part, or coming up with a way to test a circuit that narrows down which component is acting up—every day is full of little opportunities."[26]
>
> —Eugene Kozlenko, robotics engineer at Barrett Technology

Some robotics engineers specialize in one area or another. Regardless of specialty, most will spend at least some of their time troubleshooting problems and finding solutions.

Both General and Specialized Skills Are Needed

Robotics engineers need to have technical proficiency in a broad range of fields. This includes mechanical and electrical engineering, computer science, systems engineering, and more. Robotics engineers must be able to dip into knowledge from any or all of these disciplines when diagnosing a problem or envisioning a solution.

At the same time, it is also important for a robotics engineer to focus deeply on one particular area of engineering or robotics. The ideal robotics team contains engineers who each have their own distinct area of expertise yet are all familiar with the others' specialties.

Alex Owen-Hill is a writer who has a PhD in telerobotics. He says it is essential to maintain a balance between general and specialized skills. He explains:

> As specialists, we are skilled in the fine details of our specialisms. As generalists, we are able to see "the big picture"—something our broad knowledge base allows us

to do. . . . We have to be good at mechanics, electronics, electrics, programming, sensing and even psychology and cognition. A good roboticist is able to understand how all of these different systems work together and is comfortable with the theory behind all of them.[29]

Communication Skills Are Essential

Finally, all robotics engineers must be good communicators. First and foremost, they must be able to communicate well within their team of other engineers. Everyone must be on the same page about what needs to be done to improve a robot's design or fix an existing robot. "It's vital to communicate with the rest of the team, to come up with better solutions, and to be able to put the various parts of the solutions together,"[30] says Kozlenko.

However, robotics engineers must also be able to communicate very technical ideas to those who are not always familiar with them. These include salespeople, designers, and other colleagues who lack technical backgrounds but may be involved in making major decisions about the robot's design and function. Robotics engineers might also work directly with customers, who may or may not have engineering backgrounds. As such, robotics engineers must be able to explain technical issues and solutions in a way that nontechnical people can understand. They must be able to understand needs, ask appropriate questions, and provide regular updates on progress in ways that are clear and accurate yet not overly technical.

"You learn as much from what doesn't work as what does work."[28]

—Winola Lenore Rasmussen, professor at WPI and owner of Ras Labs

Since educational programs for robotics and engineering emphasize technical skills, students interested in the field may not realize the importance of writing and speaking. "Don't ignore your communications skills," says Maria Bualat, a robotics engineer at the NASA Ames Research Center. "You don't realize how much of your job is actually communicating your ideas to other people."[31]

Similarly, robotics engineers must also have good people skills, especially if they are promoted to a position that has management

Getting Your Hands Dirty

While robotics engineers spend a fair amount of time in front of a computer, they also enjoy building. Robotics technicians tend to do the majority of hands-on work with robots, including building them, repairing them, and running tests. However, robotics engineers also spend time hammering, soldering, wiring, and coding, particularly when they just want to test something out quickly. Students interested in robotics should therefore enjoy working with their hands.

Some robotics engineers love working with their hands so much they tinker with robots and other machines as a hobby outside of work. Robotics engineer Eugene Kozlenko has been tinkering ever since he created a water-powered jet ski from the parts of a water pistol and a remote-control car when he was twelve years old. "I always have two or three unfinished projects that I have lying around, just to keep my mind going," he says. "Every now and then something I've been working on for fun becomes very relevant for something I'm doing at work."

Quoted in Michelle Grottenthaler, "Rise of the Robots: Careers in Robotics," WetFeet. http://schools.wetfeet .com.

responsibilities or customer-facing duties. Mauro Togneri, a management consultant who works with technology companies, says that a lot of engineers struggle with the shift from designing things to managing workers. "I always tell people when they become managers to keep in mind that while components such as transistors have predictable behavior, people's behavior can, and will, change."[32] Paulo Younse, a robotics engineer at NASA JPL, agrees that it is essential for robotics engineers to have solid people skills. "The better you are at talking to people, working closely with them, showing them respect, helping them with their problems, and being a good leader, the better you will be at your job."[33]

What Is It Like to Work as a Robotics Engineer?

Robotics engineers work wherever people need robots. Most work at large companies that mass-produce robots, but many work at small start-up businesses on cutting edge robotics projects. Some robotics engineers work for the government on experimental robots for defense or exploration.

Robotics engineers usually work on a team composed of other engineers, technicians, and programmers. They spend their days solving problems related to a robot's design or function. Although most engineers do spend some time in a laboratory or on a factory floor doing hands-on tasks such as dismantling robots, rewiring circuits, or writing code, this type of work more often falls to others. The role of the engineer is to come up with ideas, overall designs, and solutions to problems, while technicians and programmers do the actual implementation.

Most robotics engineers work indoors in office and laboratory spaces, while others travel to assist clients. Some robotics engineers occasionally work outdoors testing or operating robots. They tend to work long hours and earn substantial salaries.

A Typical Workday

The types of problems a robotics engineer faces in a typical workday depend on the size of the company and his or her engineering specialty. At a large firm, a robotics engineer will likely specialize in a specific area of robot design, production, or maintenance. For example, Ty Tremblay works for Symbotic, a large company that produces robots for warehouses. Its customers rely on teams of two hundred to three hundred robots to drive around a warehouse gathering cartons of materials and placing them on pallets. The robots communicate with each other via a wireless network. Tremblay spends his days traveling to Symbotic customers' warehouses and making sure everything works properly. "I monitor the system and fix it if I need to," he says. Tremblay offers an example of the kind of problem he has to solve on a daily basis: "One of our warehouses was having a problem where a lot of bots were disconnecting as they drove around the warehouse." First, he gathered data and noticed that these disconnects were not related to any particular location. Plus, some bots disconnected more often than others. This led him to conclude that the problem was not with the network but with the robots

More than Just Building Robots

You might think that robotics engineers get to tinker with robots all day. But in reality, they spend a lot of time on more mundane tasks, such as attending meetings and joining conference calls. Rich Hooper is a robotics engineer at a company that designs and builds custom robots. He explains what a typical day is like for him:

[I] spend two or three hours designing electrical circuits or mechanical systems and helping younger engineers learn about these circuits and systems. . . . An hour or two working on Bills Of Materials (BOM's). . . . This is a list of all the materials in the system. It includes wires, resistors, integrated circuits, nuts, bolts and processors, etc. The manufacturing department uses the BOM's and the drawings to build the systems. [Then I spend] an hour or two in meetings or conference calls. An hour or two writing emails. An hour or two in the lab conducting experiments or trying to understand why the systems I designed are not working the way I thought they would.

Rich Hooper, "Robotics Engineer," Learn About Robots. www.learnaboutrobots.com.

themselves. "I discovered that the antennas on the bots were not designed for high vibration environments and were getting damaged internally as the bots drove around,"[34] he says. His team found a new, stronger antenna and replaced all of the bad ones.

At a smaller company or research laboratory, a robotics engineer wears more hats and contributes more to the overall development of the robot. At NASA, for example, robotics engineers tend to work on small teams and spend more hands-on time with the robots than engineers at big companies do. Paulo Younse says that he spends a few hours every day designing new parts for a robot on the computer, performing calculations, and meeting with other members of his team. He makes drawings of the parts he needs and takes them to the machine shop to be built. Later, he says, "I go into our lab to test drive some of our robots. If a robot or a robotic arm breaks, I get to disassemble it and take it to our mechanical room. Then I get to use a bunch of screwdrivers and wrenches to take it apart, figure out what's wrong, and fix it."[35] Sandeep Yayathi, a robotics engineer at NASA's Johnson Space Center, also has a lot of opportunity for hands-on work. He says, "I go from being at a desk doing design work on a computer to assembling things on a workbench right behind me and then testing those things making sure they work."[36]

> "I go from being at a desk doing design work on a computer to assembling things on a workbench right behind me and then testing those things making sure they work."[36]
>
> —Sandeep Yayathi, robotics engineer at NASA's Johnson Space Center

Working Conditions and Earnings

Robotics engineers work in many different environments. They typically spend a fair amount of time in an office going to meetings, sending e-mails to their team, doing research, analyzing data, or using programs such as MATLAB or CAD to design robots and their components. Maria Bualat, a robotics engineer at the NASA Ames Research Center, stresses that all robotics engineers spend a good amount of time each day communicating with their team. "We have engineering meetings where we'll sit

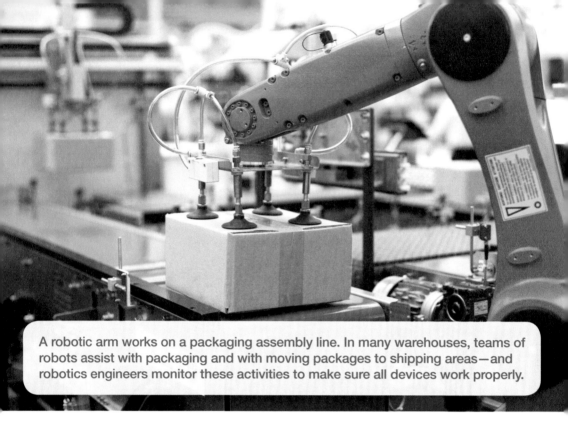

A robotic arm works on a packaging assembly line. In many warehouses, teams of robots assist with packaging and with moving packages to shipping areas—and robotics engineers monitor these activities to make sure all devices work properly.

around and brainstorm about how to solve issues that we're having, or we come up with new ideas."[37]

However, robotics engineers also spend time in laboratories, on factory floors, or even outdoors testing robots. Bualat says, "I get to do some fun stuff where I get to go out into the field. When we want to test our robots, we take them to places that are very stark and lifeless."[38] These sites are supposed to mimic the surface of another planet such as Mars, a place where a robotic rover named *Opportunity* is already exploring.

Some robotics engineers must travel to assist clients. As such, they may spend as much as a week at a time on-site with a customer, assisting with the setup of a new robot or troubleshooting issues. Even when travel is not part of the job, the work is still demanding. Most robotics engineers must work long hours in order to meet deadlines. "I usually sneak in a few hours working early in the morning on weekends," says robotics engineer and consultant Rich Hooper. "I typically work 53-hour weeks."[39]

Robotics engineers are compensated very well for their time and dedication to their work. Entry-level salaries start at around

$51,000, and the median income for a robotics engineer is $81,591, according to the website PayScale. This is approximately double the median income for all Americans. More experienced robotics engineers can expect to earn as much as $150,000 per year. These engineers also often earn bonuses or participate in profit sharing, whereby they earn money when their company does. Robotics engineers who focus on computer science can expect to earn the highest salaries, followed by those focused on electrical engineering. Mechanical engineering specialists typically earn the least, though the median income for a mechanical engineer is still quite high at $67,935.

"We have engineering meetings where we'll sit around and brainstorm about how to solve issues that we're having, or we come up with new ideas."[37]

—Maria Bualat, robotics engineer at NASA Ames Research Center

Women in Robotics

Although the number of female engineers is on the rise, men still dominate robotics and other technical fields. In 2012 the US Congress Joint Economic Committee reported that just 14 percent of all engineers in the United States were women. Though many companies are striving to increase the number of female engineers on their workforce, they often complain that there simply are not enough women graduating with the necessary skill set.

Women who may be interested in robotics face many barriers, including societal biases that engineering is more of a male pursuit or that men are better at math—both of which are untrue. Many women have become successful robotics engineers. Melonee Wise, chief operating officer (CEO) of Fetch Robotics, says, "It can be very uplifting to be a positive role model for young women who want to go into robotics. [My presence] encourages young engineers and tells them, 'Hey women have been successful, just apply yourself and work hard and barriers will move out of the way.'"[40]

The robotics industry needs more women—and more diverse employees in general—in order to develop the best products. Tessa Lau, cofounder of the robotics company Savioke, says that she looks for diversity when hiring. "It's really important, as we design our robots, to make sure they appeal to everyone—people with disabilities, minorities, people who are disadvantaged,"[41] she says. In order to make a product that appeals to diverse people, those people must be present during the design process. People from a variety of racial and cultural backgrounds, of different sexual orientations, and of varying ages all bring unique life experiences and ideas to the table at a robotics company.

Advancement and Other Job Opportunities

Because it is such an interdisciplinary field, a person with a robotics education or robotics experience will have many career options. It is actually rare to find a position simply titled "robotics engineer." Rather, engineers with a robotics education tend to focus in a specific area and advance in their careers within that area. Common specializations include mechanical engineer, controls engineer, test engineer, systems engineer, or one of many other engineering roles. With enough experience, a robotics engineer may also take on a management role and lead a team. Or he or she may spend more time working directly with clients. A seasoned robotics engineer will earn the title of senior engineer. This designates the person as an expert at the company.

As in other engineering fields, a graduate degree may be necessary to advance in your career. Engineers at a commercial robotics company may need one to two years of additional education to obtain a master's degree, while those working in design or research often need to commit several more years to obtain a doctorate. The skills a person learns as a robotics engineer tend to transfer easily to other industries, especially those in the technology sector. Since most robotics engineers are capable of designing a new robot from start to finish, they are also uniquely equipped to strike out on their own and start their own companies.

Climbing the Ladder

Climbing the corporate ladder as a robotics engineer requires dedication, people skills, and continuing education. Entry-level

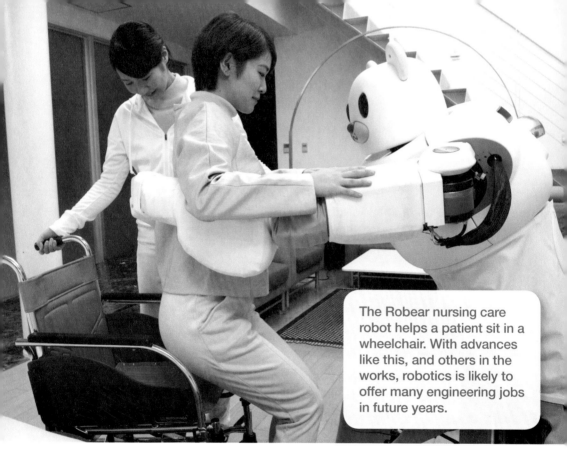

The Robear nursing care robot helps a patient sit in a wheelchair. With advances like this, and others in the works, robotics is likely to offer many engineering jobs in future years.

robotics engineers are often hired right out of college. They typically start out with job titles such as associate engineer. In this position, the new hire is like an apprentice. He or she works closely with more advanced engineers who supervise his or her work. The engineer may attend training sessions to learn more about the particular robots the company produces or maintains. "When you first graduate college, you will be a very junior engineer," says Rich Hooper. "Robots are often the most complex systems a company will make. You will need to first focus on a subsystem, such as the mechanical, electrical, computing or software systems."[42]

If an associate engineer demonstrates skill and dedication, he or she could earn a promotion within the first year or two of employment. The next job will likely be one that specializes in an aspect of robotics that matches his or her skills and experience, such as mechanical engineer or electrical engineer. At this level, the engineer will usually be responsible for a small group of technicians or programmers. For example, as a test engineer at iRobot, Corey Russell manages a testing laboratory. A technician who works for him runs the tests he devises.

From here, a robotics engineer's career takes one of two paths. The first path leads to management responsibilities. A robotics engineer may become a team leader, supervisor, or manager in charge of an entire team of engineers. He or she may also be responsible for the company's relationship with important clients. As the boss of others, the manager must organize the team's work, conduct performance reviews, keep a budget, and hire new team members. In a more management-oriented role, a robotics engineer spends more time dealing with people problems than technical ones. Ian Danforth, lead engineer at Fetch Robotics, has to squeeze his coding tasks in between interviews, meetings, and project planning. "Some days I'll have applications to go over from new candidates, sometimes I'll go through phone interviews," he says. "Then I'll do some coding before morning meetings."[43] Danforth also spends time answering his team member's questions and writing planning documents.

"When you first graduate college, you will be a very junior engineer. Robots are often the most complex systems a company will make. You will need to first focus on a subsystem, such as the mechanical, electrical, computing or software systems."[42]

—Rich Hooper, robotics engineer

The second career path is to garner expertise in an engineering specialty and in the company's main product. After five to ten years of experience, the person will become a senior engineer. In this position, he or she will continue to work on robots but will take responsibility for larger, more high-profile projects and will often mentor newer engineers.

A Variety of Career Options

It is hard to think of a job that is cooler than working with robots. However, not all robotics engineers stay in the field for their whole careers. The interdisciplinary skills required to work with robots

Staying Sharp

Robotics engineers must constantly update and refresh their skills. They must be enthusiastic about learning new programming languages, revolutionary technologies, and novel approaches to the field. Keeping technology skills sharp takes time and effort and may require additional education, even a master's degree or PhD.

Professional organizations can also provide technical and interpersonal training for robotics engineers. These organizations may help people network to find mentors or provide certifications in a variety of engineering specialties. While certification is not necessary to work as a robotics engineer, it could help you stand out compared to other engineers who are not certified. In addition to the Institute of Electrical and Electronics Engineers, the American Society for Engineering Education and the American Society of Mechanical Engineers are excellent resources for robotics engineers.

come in handy in a variety of other technical industries. A robotics engineer could end up working in telecommunications, electronics, software, or technology for the medical or energy industries.

Consumer electronics is an exciting field for robotics engineers to move into. Cell phones, tablets, and smart watches are not robots . . . technically. The only real difference is that these gadgets do not move on their own. However, their electrical and software systems share a lot of common features with robots.

Similarly, the software engineering industry is a great match for people who have robotics experience. Computer programming is an essential skill that robotics engineers must develop. Opportunities in software engineering go far beyond robotics to include everything from mobile applications to video games and artificial intelligence.

In the biomedical industry, engineers develop technology for doctors, surgeons, and others in the health care industry to use. While robotics is a huge part of this field, these engineers also develop diagnostic equipment, artificial organs, and more. Robotics is also important in the energy industry, which offers opportunities for people with technical skills to develop underground 3D mapping software, batteries, fuel cells, solar panels, wind turbines, and more.

Academia and Entrepreneurship

Finally, robotics engineers who have advanced degrees may choose to work in academia as professors at colleges or universities. There they can pursue their own research interests while teaching and mentoring students. A successful research project may lead to the opportunity to start a business. For example, Rodney Brooks began his career at MIT as director of the institute's Computer Science and Artificial Intelligence Laboratory. From there, he went on to found two robotics companies, iRobot and Rethink Robotics. Brooks says that moving from academia to industry requires that one learn to focus on the customer's needs. "In academia, it's the technology, the science or idea which is valued," he says. But customers do not necessarily care about the science. "It's valued by the customer if something works, does the job, is cheaper and better, and it doesn't matter what the technology is to them."[44]

"In academia, it's the technology, the science or idea which is valued."[44]

—Rodney Brooks, founder of iRobot and Rethink Robotics

As an entrepreneur, a robotics engineer must become even more versatile than normal. He or she must also be able to sell the idea behind the new company to potential investors and customers and be able to build a team of people to successfully run the business.

CHAPTER 6

What Does the Future Hold for Robotics Engineers?

The field of robotics is growing, thanks to major advances in technology. Robots already scout out the deep oceans and distant planets, and they will continue to explore the unknown in the future. Driverless cars already share the roads with regular cars and trucks and will only become more common. Robotic drones will deliver packages. Flexible robots will perform simple surgeries. Search-and-rescue robots will save people from disasters. Robots may even become our friends and assistants as they help children learn, entertain us, care for the elderly, and complete chores around the home. In any industry that builds or uses robots, engineers are needed.

Many engineers go into robotics because of the field's great potential to improve people's lives. This is what inspired M. Bernardine Dias of the Robotics Institute at Carnegie Mellon University to enter the field. "I was drawn to the field of robotics because it provided a great opportunity to invent a future where technology can assist humankind in numerous ways," Dias says. "Imagining a better future for all, and making that future a reality is definitely an incredibly exciting career path."[45]

A Competitive Field

In the United States the number of jobs for robotics engineers is expected to increase 5 percent through 2024, a rate that is slightly slower than average, according to the Bureau of Labor Statistics (BLS). However, the BLS groups robotics engineers under mechanical engineers, a profession that mainly finds work in manufacturing. While robotics as an industry is growing worldwide, manufacturing in the United States has been diminishing, and many manufacturing operations are moving overseas. In addition, the automotive industry, a huge market for robotics, was hit hard by the economic recession in 2008. These facts partially account for the predicted slow rate of growth in mechanical and robotics engineering jobs.

Though many experts predict that jobs in robotics will grow more quickly than in other industries, robotics engineers may want to play it safe and plan for a competitive hiring environment, especially in manufacturing and industrial robotics. Those who obtain advanced degrees or specialize in software engineering or medical robotics will have an easier time finding a job. For example, the BLS predicts 17 percent job growth for software engineers and 23 percent job growth for biomedical engineers through 2024.

> "I was drawn to the field of robotics because it provided a great opportunity to invent a future where technology can assist humankind in numerous ways. Imagining a better future for all, and making that future a reality is definitely an incredibly exciting career path."[45]
>
> —M. Bernardine Dias, professor at the Robotics Institute, Carnegie Mellon University

Beyond Manufacturing

Robots are not just for manufacturing anymore. They are popping up everywhere. Sonia Chernova, a professor at the Georgia Institute of Technology, predicts, "Career options in robotics will grow tremendously in the coming years!"[46] According to her, robots are on the cusp of entering the everyday lives of millions of people through advances such as self-driving cars, cleaning robots, and flying delivery drones. The market for service robots, or robots that do everything besides manufacturing, is expected to grow 17.8 percent between 2015 and 2020, according to a report from Zion Marketing Research.

Medicine is another tremendous area of interest for robotics, says Chernova. There are potential applications in prosthetics, autonomous wheelchairs, smart homes, rehabilitation, and surgery. People are living longer around the world, but the job of caring for elderly patients is physically demanding and often does not pay very well. This is one reason why robots will become an essential part of health care. Bill Townsend, CEO of Barrett Technology, predicts that society will see more robots in health services in coming years. "Over the next ten years, robots will be overlapping workspaces with people and working in assisted-living areas, hospitals, and rehabilitation centers, working literally hand in hand with people,"[47] he says. Many care facilities already use robots to assist the elderly. For example, the robot Robear is a mechanical caregiver developed by the Japanese research institute Riken. It can lift and carry patients. PARO is a brand of robot that looks like a cuddly baby seal and is meant to provide comfort and companionship.

Artificial Intelligence

In order to provide the care that elderly patients need, robots will have to get smarter. They will need to be able to see and recognize objects and people in the environment, and they will have to prioritize a lot of different duties. To perform complex tasks and work with people, robots need to possess artificial intelligence, or software that allows them to act autonomously and make their own decisions. Chris Jones, director of research advancement for iRobot, predicts that there will be a lot of growth in smart robotics. "We are going to start seeing more sophistication and increased capabilities being put into robots through the addition of intelligent software,"[48] he says.

Advances in artificial intelligence will impact every industry in which robots play a role. In manufacturing, robots will no longer need to be caged for safety and will work side by side with people. People will be able to train robots simply by demonstrating a task; the robot will simply watch and learn. In the transportation industry, self-driving cars will likely replace regular cars and self-flying drones could become familiar sites in the skies as they deliver packages or collect data. In homes, robots will fold laundry, clean, and cook. In space, the deep sea, and disaster situations, smart robots will be able to explore dangerous environments on their own, with fewer step-by-step instructions from human operators.

For all of these reasons, Erik Nieves describes future robots

Ethical Robots

A lot of progress needs to be made before a robot can interact with a person with the same friendliness and adaptability as a human nurse, but researchers are taking steps toward this goal. Susan and Michael Anderson, a husband-and-wife team of researchers at the University of Connecticut and the University of Hartford, are working on a software system to give a medical robot a sense of ethics to help it choose the correct action to take at any given time.

The first version of their system brought medication to patients. If the patient refused to take it, the robot would balance the harm that might come to the patient from not taking the medicine against the patient's right to refuse. It then made a decision about whether to alert a doctor or leave the patient alone. The next version of the robot will know when to charge itself and will monitor patients in its care. "It's also going to watch to see if a person has been persistently immobile for a while," says Michael Anderson. In this situation, it will attempt to engage the person and notify an overseer if there is no response. In the future, health care robots will also be able to bathe patients, play games with them, and even hold conversations.

Michael Anderson and Susan Anderson, interview with the author, July 20, 2016.

as almost human in their ability to interact with the world. "They're going to have vision systems and cameras to tell them where they are in space," he says. "They're going to have a sense of touch. They're going to have an ability to make sure that they're not interfering with obstacles in their path. There are all kinds of sensory technologies that are being incorporated into robots. That's really going to be the robot of tomorrow."[49]

However, even these advanced humanoid robots will not be able to replace human friends and family. Rather, robots of the future will allow people to focus more energy and attention on creative tasks and human connection. Pamela Rutledge, director of

Already widespread in manufacturing, robots are poised to become a part of everyday life in areas ranging from package delivery to medicine. As the field grows, so will competition for engineering jobs in all areas of robotics.

the Media Psychology Research Center, says that machines will not be able to perform tasks and services that require thought, creativity, problem solving, and innovation. Rather, advanced robots and computer programs will take over repetitive, boring, and dangerous tasks, allowing people to spend their time on areas where a more human approach is required. These areas include social work, government, education, entrepreneurship, and the creation of art. Rutledge says, "We already have cars that talk to us, a phone we can talk to, robots that lift the elderly out of bed, and apps that remind us to call Mom. An app can dial Mom's number and even send flowers, but an app can't do that most human of all things: emotionally connect with her."[50]

Robot Overlords?

Some worry that advanced or intelligent robots will force people out of their jobs. For example, driverless cars could take the place of human taxi drivers, bus drivers, and truck drivers. However, in the past, new technology has always created new jobs to replace the ones that are no longer needed. Vint Cerf, vice president of Google, says, "Historically, technology has created more jobs than it destroys," He says there is no reason to think robotics technology will be any different. "Someone has to make and service all these advanced devices,"[51] he explains. In the case of robots, that someone is a robotics engineer or technician. If you work in robotics, your job is safe, says Ty Tremblay, a field systems engineer at Symbotic. "You will never have your industry disappear in your lifetime."[52]

Others are concerned that computers or robots will become even smarter than humans. Such superintelligent machines could potentially decide to rule the world or even exterminate humanity, as is forewarned in science fiction movies such as *The Matrix*. To avoid this scenario, robotics engineers and scientists must be sure to consider the safety and ethical impacts of their projects. In 2015 a group of prominent scientists, including Stephen Hawking, all signed a letter imploring robotics and artificial intelligence researchers to avoid creating something that cannot be controlled. Though the robots engineers are building now are not smart enough to pose a real risk—and will not be for a long time—safeguards that researchers take now could matter in the future.

Instead of worrying that robots will compete with people for jobs or take over completely, it is more realistic—and productive—to imagine robots and people joining forces to make the world a better place. "We are already becoming one with our machines and devices—and those integrations are only going to become deeper," predicts Paul Berberian. He is CEO of the robotics company Sphero, which makes a robotic

> "We are already becoming one with our machines and devices—and those integrations are only going to become deeper."[53]
>
> —Paul Berberian, CEO of Sphero

toy that looks like BB-8 from *Star Wars*. "Machines are now with us for most of our days and lives," says Berberian. "In the future, there will be more of them. Many will be temporary or for special purposes, and some for utility, but a lot for entertainment."[53]

Many people already carry cell phones and tablets everywhere. One day in the not-too-distant future, robots will likely join the list of must-have gadgets. Society will rely on these intelligent machines for everything from health care to entertainment. And who will be behind the scenes imagining, designing, and producing them? Robotics engineers.

CHAPTER 7

Interview with a Robotics Engineer

Corey Russell received his master of science degree in robotics engineering from WPI in 2013. He now works at iRobot, a company that designs and sells vacuum-cleaning and mopping robots for use in the home. He spoke with the author about his career.

Q: Why did you become a robotics engineer?

A: Because it was awesome! In college, I was studying to be a mechanical engineer because I really liked math and physics. But I wasn't enjoying it as much as I thought I was going to. My school happened to have a robotics program, so I took the introductory course and fell in love with it.

A robotics engineer is a combination of four engineers, with the skills of a mechanical engineer, a software engineer, an electrical engineer, and a systems engineer all wrapped up in one person.

Q: Your job at iRobot is test engineer. Why isn't your title robotics engineer?

A: Robotics as an industry is growing very quickly, but a lot of employers haven't caught on yet that they need robotics engineers. But I think that's beginning to change. At iRobot, we do have robotics engineers. We also have electrical engineers, mechanical engineers, software engineers, and systems engineers who make sure everything fits together.

Robotics engineers get tasked with a lot of really challenging problems that require all the knowledge that comes with being a robotics engineer. They build theories and come up with ideas to get a project to a starting point, then they hand it off to people who are a little more specialized to do a lot of the rest of the work.

People with robotics education would love to end up in a robotics engineer position, but those are super rare. So a lot of us end up taking the next best thing, whatever will get us close to robotics so we can build up and use the unique education we have.

Q: Can you describe your typical workday?

A: We have a realistic lab environment in the building and I run that entire lab. Before any robot gets released, it goes through me to make sure the whole thing works. I'm one of the people giving a thumbs up or thumbs down for whether or not it's ready to go.

Typically, someone comes to us and says, "We're in a pretty good spot right now, everything's working. Can you tell us how we're doing?" They hand off the robot, and we come up with tests we can run to figure out how well it's working or what parts need improvement. We run those tests and then we work with the engineering teams to figure out what issues we have and suggest solutions.

I have a technician who works underneath me, and he's the one actually running the tests. These tests usually involve watching the robot, and making sure it behaves like a smart robot should. For example, we want to make sure that the robot knows what a chair leg is and what to do around it, where the stairwell is and not to drive off of it, and that the robot doesn't get stuck on things that people have in their home. On any given day, the technician will be running around, starting robots here and there, recording what happens, taking notes on it, and collecting data from the robot when it finishes. I'll also have a whole bunch of meetings with different engineers on different teams translating test results into what needs to happen next.

For example, a robot might keep getting stuck in one certain part of the lab. Let's say it can't handle a certain type of flooring. I'll gather enough results to say: "We're having a problem doing this. Here's why I think that problem exists, and here's what we can do to fix it." I do a lot of data reporting and data analysis from everything that I gather.

I have worked with both of the most recent releases from iRobot. The BraavaJet 240 is a nifty little robot that sweeps and mops your floors, and drives in straight lines to clean just like a normal person would. The Roomba 980 is a vacuuming robot that will clean an entire floor, and map your house while it's cleaning so it won't miss anything—it's the smartest Roomba we've ever made.

Q: What do you like most about your job?
A: I meet all sorts of people who are way smarter than me. As crazy as it can be, every day I learn something new. For somebody with an engineering background, that's like candy.

Q: What do you like least about your job?
A: One of the things I like least about my job is how hectic it can get during the day. My job requires me to do many different things, and sometimes I have to do all of them at once. For instance, I've had days where I have to write some code, manage some interns doing work, write some reports, go to meetings, check the machine shop for parts, watch some robots, and help people debug issues all at once. It's really easy for the day to get away from you and leave without feeling like you accomplished anything.

Q: What personal qualities do you find most valuable for this type of work?
A: You have to have a lot of drive and really care about what you're doing. Stuff changes so rapidly and there are so many moving parts that every so often you've got to pull several 16-hour days in a row to get everything done in time. If you don't love what you're doing, that's not going to go well.

Q: What advice do you have for students who might be interested in this career?
A: Get involved early. There are a lot of programs for kids in middle school and high school, including FIRST Robotics and VEX Robotics. But if your school doesn't have those programs, then buy an Arduino. It's a little control board with its own software environment, and it's a great first tool for anything in the robotics

industry. It gets you learning and developing skills that will become invaluable later on in a tech environment.

Q: What does the future hold for robotics engineering?

A: It's a growing industry that we haven't fully developed yet. We're advancing so incredibly quickly that I have no idea where we're going to end up in ten years. I get the feeling that people with a robotics background are always going to be useful, especially as more and more things in our world become automated and have robotics systems in them. If you had said five years ago that some of the robotics systems we have today were going to exist, people would have laughed at you.

At iRobot, we have a good amount of insight into what people expect out of robots in the home. It's a high standard to live up to, but more and more home automation is coming—not only from us, but from everybody else in the industry. It's what people want nowadays. Everything is getting smarter.

Q: Are you happy with your career choice?

A: Yes. It's a lot of long hours and the work is very hard, but it's very fulfilling. I have the opportunity to play with cool things every day—not a whole lot of other people get to do that. It's a lot of fun! Plus, my roommates love me. Within eyesight, I have six Roombas and five of the BraavaJet 240s. We have a very clean floor!

SOURCE NOTES

Introduction: Turning Science Fiction into Reality

1. Alex Knapp, "The Top Majors for the Class of 2022," *Forbes*, May 9, 2012. www.forbes.com.
2. Knapp, "The Top Majors for the Class of 2022."
3. Quoted in Michelle Grottenthaler, "Rise of the Robots: Careers in Robotics," WetFeet. http://schools.wetfeet.com.
4. Erik Nieves, "Engineering Your Future—Robotics Engineer," ThinkTVPBS, January 29, 2009. www.youtube.com/watch?v=umNfDhi0kB0.
5. Bill Gates, "A Robot in Every Home," *Scientific American*, January 1, 2007. www.scientificamerican.com.
6. Chris Jones, "Dr. Chris Jones, Director for Research Advancement at iRobot," KidsAhead, October 29, 2012. http://kidsahead.com.
7. Anne Fisher, "Revenge of the Robotics Nerds: They're In Demand," *Fortune*, March 20, 2012. http://fortune.com.
8. Quoted in Imagiverse, "An Interview with Paulo Younse," May 19, 2006. http://imagiverse.org.

Chapter 1: What Does a Robotics Engineer Do?

9. Quoted in Jennifer Kimrey, "Mechanical, Robotics Engineers See Demand," *Chron*, January 31, 2014. www.chron.com.
10. Timothy Hay, "The Robots Are Coming to Hospitals," *Wall Street Journal*, March 15, 2012. www.wsj.com.
11. Ayanna Howard, "Robotics Engineer," Gigniks, August 17, 2013. www.youtube.com/watch?v=ihOsdC85-gc.
12. David Wethe, "Robots: The Future of the Oil Industry," Bloomberg, August 30, 2012. www.bloomberg.com.

Chapter 2: How Do You Become a Robotics Engineer?

13. Nieves, "Engineering Your Future—Robotics Engineer."
14. Nieves, "Engineering Your Future—Robotics Engineer."
15. Alex Owen-Hill, "10 Essential Skills That All Good Roboticists Should Have," *Robotiq* (blog), January 5, 2016. http://blog.robotiq.com.

16. Quoted in Kimrey, "Mechanical, Robotics Engineers See Demand."
17. Rich Hooper, "Robotics Engineer," Learn About Robots. www.learnaboutrobots.com.
18. Quoted in Ashley, "Roboticists Answer Our Questions," NASA. https://robotics.nasa.gov.
19. Joseph St. Germain, interview with the author, June 11, 2016.
20. Quoted in NASA, "Arin Morfopoulos— Robotics Engineer," November 19, 2009. www.nasa.gov.
21. Quoted in NASA, "Fernando Zumbado—Robotics Systems Engineer," November 9, 2009. www.nasa.gov.
22. Ty Tremblay, interview with the author, June 21, 2016.
23. Quoted in Jane (J.M.) Bedell, *So, You Want to Be a Coder?* New York: Aladdin, 2016, p. 176.
24. Quoted in Ashley, "Roboticists Answer Our Questions."

Chapter 3: What Skills and Personal Qualities Matter Most—and Why?

25. Corey Russell, interview with the author, June 24, 2016.
26. Quoted in Grottenthaler, "Rise of the Robots."
27. Quoted in Grottenthaler, "Rise of the Robots."
28. Winola Lenore Rasmussen, interview with the author, June 11, 2016.
29. Owen-Hill, "10 Essential Skills That All Good Roboticists Should Have."
30. Quoted in Grottenthaler, "Rise of the Robots."
31. Maria Bualat, "Career Spotlight: Robotics Engineer," KQED Quest, September 28, 2015. www.youtube.com/watch?v=sUOY3JZ-9C4.
32. Quoted in Stephen Cass, "From Engineer to Manager: How to Cope with Promotion," *IEEE Spectrum*, April 21 2015. http://spectrum.ieee.org.
33. Quoted in Imagiverse, "An Interview with Paulo Younse."

Chapter 4: What Is It like to Work as a Robotics Engineer?

34. Tremblay, interview.
35. Quoted in Imagiverse, "An Interview with Paulo Younse."
36. Sandeep Yayathi, "Mission: Solar System—Sandeep Yayathi,

Robotics Engineer," Design Squad, June 11, 2013. www. youtube.com/watch?v=bhVQDGUz2Fo.

37. Bualat, "Career Spotlight."
38. Bualat, "Career Spotlight."
39. Hooper, "Robotics Engineer."
40. Quoted in Lauren Orsini, "What It Took These Four Women to Get into Robotics," *ReadWrite* (blog), March 10, 2015. http: //readwrite.com.
41. Tessa Lau, "Day in the Life: Robotics Engineer," ConnectEd Studios, March 9, 2016. www.youtube.com/watch?v=7trO3 sQzmf8.

Chapter 5: Advancement and Other Job Opportunities

42. Hooper, "Robotics Engineer."
43. Quoted in Muse, "Meet Fetch Robotics' Ian Danforth," 2017. www.themuse.com.
44. Quoted in Joanne Pransky, "The Essential Interview: Rodney Brooks, Founder of Rethink Robotics," *Robotics Business Review*, February 12, 2015. www.roboticsbusinessreview .com.

Chapter 6: What Does the Future Hold for Robotics Engineers?

45. Quoted in *International Journal of Advanced Robotic Systems*, "Women in Robotics," 2015. www.intechopen.com.
46. Quoted in Jane (J.M.) Bedell, *So, You Want to Be a Coder?* New York: Aladdin, 2016, p. 185.
47. Quoted in Grottenthaler, "Rise of the Robots."
48. Jones, "Dr. Chris Jones, Director for Research Advancement at iRobot."
49. Nieves, "Engineering Your Future—Robotics Engineer."
50. Quoted in Aaron Smith and Janna Anderson, "AI, Robotics, and the Future of Jobs," Pew Research Center, August 6, 2014. www.pewinternet.org.
51. Quoted in Smith and Anderson, "AI, Robotics, and the Future of Jobs."
52. Tremblay, interview.
53. Quoted in Stephanie Walden, "CES: Beyond the Tech," Mashable, January 7, 2016. http://mashable.com.

FIND OUT MORE

American Society for Engineering Education (ASEE)

1818 N St. NW, Suite 600
Washington, DC 20036-2479
www.asee.org

ASEE promotes education in engineering worldwide. It supports activities that increase student enrollment at engineering colleges and universities and fosters communication about teaching engineering among educational institutions, corporations, and governments. Members include engineering students, faculty, administrators, and professionals.

American Society of Mechanical Engineers (ASME)

2 Park Ave.
New York, NY 10016
www.asme.org

ASME welcomes all mechanical engineers, including robotics engineers. Members get access to conferences, competitions, journals, and more resources for advancing their careers. ASME programs support K–12 science, technology, engineering, and mathematics education; engineering and global development projects; student and early-career engineers; and public policy programs.

EngineerGirl

National Academy of Engineering
500 Fifth St. NW, Room 1047
Washington, DC 20001
www.engineergirl.org

Created by the National Academy of Engineering, the Engineer-Girl website is designed to bring national attention to the exciting opportunities that engineering represents for girls and women.

It features short profiles of 294 female engineers, dozens of in-depth interviews, and sections titled "Ask an Engineer," "Day in the Life," and "Historical Engineers."

FIRST

200 Bedford St.
Manchester, NH 03101
www.firstinspires.org

For Inspiration and Recognition of Science and Technology sponsors the FIRST Robotics Competition, which involves student-built robots competing against each other. The competition challenges participants to solve problems that involve science, technology, engineering, and math. FIRST LEGO League offers similar competitions for elementary and middle school students.

International Federation of Robotics (IFR)

Lyoner Str. 18
60528 Frankfurt am Main
Germany
www.ifr.org

The IFR seeks to promote and strengthen the robotics industry worldwide and to increase public awareness of robotics technologies.

Robotics and Automation Society (RAS)

445 Hoes Lane
Piscataway Township, NJ 08854
www.ieee-ras.org

The RAS is a group within the Institute of Electrical and Electronics Engineers that promotes the exchange of scientific and technical knowledge in robotics and automation. Through journals, newsletters, and meetings, the group spreads news, facilitates research, and documents best practices in the robotics industry.

Robotics Education & Competition Foundation

PO Box 8276
Greenville, TX 75404
www.roboticseducation.org

This organization gets students more interested and involved in science, technology, engineering, and mathematics through robotics competitions, including VEX, TSA, and BEST Robotics.

PICTURE CREDITS

Cover: iStockphoto/zoranm

6: Maury Aaseng

9: Associated Press

12: iStockphoto/zoranm

19: Hill Street Studios Blend Images/Newscom

28: iStockphoto/nd3000

34: iStockphoto/wellphoto

38: Associated Press

46: iStockphoto/Oktay Ortakcioglu

Kathryn Hulick is a freelance writer, editor, and former Peace Corps volunteer. She lives in Massachusetts with her husband and son. They like to hike, read, cook, garden, visit the ocean, and play with their dog, Maya. Hulick contributes regularly to *Muse* magazine and the Science News for Students website. She has written many books and articles for children, about everything from outer space to video games. Her book *High Tech Careers: Careers in Robotics* came out in 2017.